MIRACLES AND SUPERNATURAL RELIGION

BIBLICAL NARRATIVES

First Edition 1903
James Morris Whiton PhD

New Edition 2019
Edited by Tarl Warwick

COPYRIGHT AND DISCLAIMER

FOREWORD

"Miracles and Supernatural Religions" is a fairly in depth but rather short study of the concept of miracles within a Christian context, broken apart into numerous sections each with their own particular philosophical goals and backing scripture- Whiton makes sure to include a variety of secondary sources alongside the Christian Bible itself in order to illustrate the points that he makes- especially with regards to the miracle (found in the bible and in rationalistic works alike) of the resuscitation of dead bodies back to life, as in the story of Lazarus.

Some of these secondary resources strictly endorse the concept, especially with regards to accidental burials involving people merely cataleptic, among other things, that is, which are not actually dead at all. Indeed, the concept of miracles as detached from these more rationalistic meanderings is here skeptically regarded to an extent, although it is clear that the writer was indeed a practicing Christian.

This edition of "Miracles and Supernatural Religion" has been carefully edited for content and format. Care has been taken to retain all original intent and meaning. A great deal of archaic language was modernized during the process where possible to substitute an exact modern equivalent.

MIRACLES AND SUPERNATURAL RELIGION

PREFATORY NOTE

While the present subject of discussion tempts to many an excursion into particulars, its treatment is restricted to general outlines, with an aim simply to clarify current ideas of miracle and the supernatural, so as to find firm holding ground for tenable positions in the present "drift period" of theology. The chief exception made to this general treatment is the discussion given to a class of miracles regarded with as much incredulity as any, yet as capable as any of being accredited as probably historical events the raisings of the "dead." The insistence of some writers on the virgin birth and corporeal resurrection of Jesus as essential to Christianity has required brief discussion of these also, mainly with reference to the reasonableness of that demand. As to the latter miracle, it must be observed that in the Biblical narratives taken as a whole, whichever of their discordant features one be disposed to emphasize, the psychical element clearly preponderates over the physical and material.

J. M. W.
New York, April 11, 1903.

MIRACLES AND SUPERNATURAL RELIGION

INTRODUCTORY

In a historical retrospect greater and more revolutionary changes are seen to have occurred during the nineteenth century than in any century preceding. In these changes no department of thought and activity has failed to share, and theological thought has been quite as much affected as scientific or ethical. Especially remarkable is the changed front of Christian theologians toward miracles, their distinctly lowered estimate of the significance of miracle, their antipodal reverse of the long established treatment of miracles. Referring to this a British evangelical writer (Professor W.T. Adeney in the *Hibbert Journal,* January 1903, p. 302) observes that "the intelligent believer of our own day... instead of accepting Christianity on the ground of the miracles, accepts it in spite of the miracles. Whether he admits these miracles, or rejects them, his attitude toward them is toward difficulties, not helps." By this diametrical change of Christian thought a great amount of skepticism has already been antiquated. A once famous anti-Christian book, *Supernatural Religion*, regarded as formidable thirty years ago, is now as much out of date for relevancy to present theological conditions as is the old smooth-bore cannon for naval warfare. That many, indeed, are still unaware of the change that has been experienced by the leaders of Christian thought, no one acquainted with current discussions will deny; the fact is indubitable.

It is reviewed in the following pages with the constructive purpose of redeeming the idea of supernatural Religion from pernicious perversion, and of exhibiting it in its true spiritual significance. The once highly reputed calculations made to show how the earth's diurnal revolution could be imperceptibly stopped for Joshua's convenience, and the contention that the Mediterranean produced fish with gullets capable of giving passage to Jonah, are now as dead as the chemical controversy about phlogiston. Yet some skeptical controversialists are still so far from cultivating the acquaintance with recent thought which they recommend to Christian theologians, as to persist in affirmations of amazing ignorance, e.g. "It is admitted that miracles alone can attest the reality of divine revelation." (See the recent new edition of *Supernatural Religion*, 'carefully revised.')

Sponsors for this statement must now be sought among unlearned Christians, or among a few scholars who survive as cultivators of the old-fashioned argument from the "evidences." Even among these latter the tendency to minimize miracle is undeniably apparent in a reduction of the list classified as such, and still more in the brevity of the list insisted on for the attestation of Christianity. A transitional state of mind is clearly evidenced by the present division and perplexity of Christian thought concerning the Christian miracles. Many seem to regard further discussion as profitless, and are ready to shelve the subject. But this attitude of weariness is also transitional. There must be some thoroughfare to firm ground and clear vision. It must be found in agreement, first of all, on the real meaning of a term so variously and vaguely used as miracle. In the present imperfect state of knowledge it may be impossible to enucleate miracle, however defined, of all mystery. But even so will much be gained for clear thinking, if miracle can be reasonably related to the greater mystery which all accept, though none understand, the mystery of life. This view of the dynamic relation of life to miracle (For an earlier statement of this by the present writer, see a discourse on 'Miracle and Life,' in *New Points to Old Texts*. London; James Clarke & Co., 1889. New York: Thomas Whittaker.) is here suggested for what it may prove to be worth.

The great and general change that transfigured theology during the nineteenth century was characteristically ethical. This, indeed, is the distinctive feature of the so-called new theology, in contrast with that which the Protestant Reformers inherited from St. Augustine. God and Man, Faith, Salvation and Inspiration, Redemption and Atonement, Judgment and Retribution, all these themes are now presented in orthodox pulpits far more conformably to ethical principles, though in degrees varying with educated intelligence, than was customary in the sermons of half a century ago. "One great source and spring of theological progress," says Professor Bowne, in his recent work on Theism, "has been the need of finding a conception of God which the moral nature could accept. The necessity of moralizing theology has produced vast changes in that field; and the end is not yet."

The ethical character of the theological change will perhaps be most obvious in the field of Biblical study, to which the present subject belongs. The traditional solution of such moral difficulties in the Old Testament as commands, ostensibly divine, to massacre idolaters has been quite discarded.

It is no longer the mode to say that deeds seemingly atrocious were not atrocious, because God commanded them. Writers of orthodox repute now say that the Thus saith the Lord, with which Samuel prefaced his order to exterminate the Amalekites, must be understood subjectively, as an expression of the prophet's belief, not objectively, as a divine command communicated to him. This great change is a quite recent change. If a personal reference may be indulged, it is not twenty years since the present writer's published protest against "The Anti-Christian Use of the Bible in the Sunday School," (*The New Englander*, September, 1884.) the exhibition to children of some vestiges of heathen superstition embedded in the Old Testament narratives as true illustrations of God's ways toward men, drew forth from a religious journal a bitter editorial on "The Old Testament and its New Enemies." But a great light has since dawned in that quarter. It is no longer deemed subversive of faith in a divine Revelation to hold that the prophet Gad was not infallible in regarding the plague which scourged Jerusalem as sent to punish David's pride in his census of the nation.

A significant fact is presented in the comparison of these two aspects of the theological change that has come to pass, the growing importance of the ethical, and the dwindling importance of the miraculous in the religious thought of today. This may reassure those who fear whereto such change may grow. The inner significance of such a change is most auspicious. It portends the displacement of a false by the true conception of supernatural Religion, and the removal thereby of a serious antagonism between Science and Christian Theology, as well as of a serious hindrance of many thoughtful minds from an intelligent embrace of Christianity.

MIRACLES AND SUPERNATURAL RELIGION

SECTION I

SYNOPSIS: The gradual narrowing of the miraculous element in the Bible by recent discovery and discussion. The alarm thereby excited in the Church. The fallacy which generates the fear. The atheistic conception of nature which generates the fallacy. The present outgrowing of this conception.

It is barely forty years since that beloved and fearless Christian scholar, Dean Stanley, spoke thus of the miracles recorded of the prophet Elisha: "His works stand alone in the Bible in their likeness to the acts of medieval saints. There alone in the Sacred History the gulf between Biblical and Ecclesiastical miracles almost disappears." (Lectures on the *History of the Jewish Church,* Vol. II, p. 362, American edition.) It required some courage to say as much as this then, while the storm of persecution was raging against Bishop Colenso for his critical work on the Pentateuch.

The evangelical clergymen in England and the United States then prepared to confess as much as this, with all that it obviously implies, could have been seated in a small room. But time has moved on, and the Church, at least the scholars of the Church, have moved with it. No scholar of more than narrowly local repute now hesitates to acknowledge the presence of a legendary element both in the Old Testament and in the New. While the extent of it is still undetermined, many specimens of it are recognized. It is agreed that the early narratives in Genesis are of this character, and that it is marked in such stories as those of Samson, Elijah, and Elisha. Even the conservative revisers of the Authorized Version have eliminated from the Fourth Gospel story of the angel at the pool of Bethesda, and in their marginal notes on the Third Gospel have admitted a doubt concerning the historicity of the angel and the bloody sweat in

9

MIRACLES AND SUPERNATURAL RELIGION

Gethsemane.

Furthermore, some events, recognized as historical, have been divested of the miraculous character once attributed to them, the crossing of the Red Sea, for instance, by the Hebrew host. A landslip in the thirteenth century A.D. has been noted as giving historical character to the story of the Hebrew host under Joshua's command crossing the Jordan "on dry ground" but in a perfectly natural way. Other classes of phenomena once regarded as miraculous have been transferred to the domain of natural processes by the investigations and discoveries that have been made in the field of psychical research.

The forewarning which God is said to have given the prophet Elijah of the visit that the queen was about to pay him in disguise (Kings xiv. 1-7.) is now recognized as one of many cases of the mysterious natural function that we label as "telepathy." The transformations of unruly, vicious, and mentally disordered characters by hypnotic influence that have been effected at the Saltpetriere in Paris, and elsewhere, by physicians expert in psychical therapeutics are closely analogous to the cures wrought by Jesus on some victims of "demoniac possession." (It is not intended to intimate that there is no such darker reality as a "possession" that is "demoniac" indeed. It cannot be reasonably pronounced superstitious to judge that there is some probability for that view. At any rate, it is certain that the problem is not to be settled by dogmatic pronouncement. It is certain, also, that the burden of proof rests on those who contend that there can be no such thing. On the other hand, it may be conceded that the cases recorded in the New Testament do not seem to be of an essentially devilish kind. On the general subject of "possession" see F. W. H. Myers's work on *Human Personality and Survival after Death*, Vol. I. (Longmans, Green & Co., New York and London.) Professor William James half humorously remarks; "The time honored phenomenon of diabolical possession is on the point of being admitted by the scientist as a fact, now that he has the name of hysterodemonopathy by which to perceive it." *Varieties of Religious Experience*, p. 501, note.)

The cases of apparition (See *Dictionary of Psychology*, art. "Psychical Research.") also, which have been investigated and verified by the Society for Psychical Research have laid a solid basis of fact for the Biblical stories of angels, as at least, a class of phenomena to be regarded as by no means altogether legendary, but having their place among natural though mysterious occurrences. But this progressive paring down of the miraculous element in the Bible has caused outcries of unfeigned alarm. Christian scholars who have taken part in it are reproached as deserters to the camp of unbelief. They are accused of banishing God from his world, and of reducing the course of events to an order of agencies quite undivine. "Miracle" writes one of these brethren, (Dr. Peloubet, *Teachers Commentary on the Acts*, 1902.) "is the personal intervention of God into the chain of cause and effect." But what does this mean, except that, when no miracles occur, God is not personally, i.e. actively, in the chain of natural causes and effects? As Professor Drummond says; "If God appears periodically, he disappears periodically." It is precisely this view of the subject that really banishes God from his world. Those who thus define miracle regard miracles as having ceased at the end of the Apostolic age in the first century. Except, therefore, for the narrow range of human history that the Bible covers in time and place, God has not been personally in the chain of natural causes and effects. Thus close to an atheistic conception of nature does zeal for traditional orthodoxy unwittingly but really come.

The first pages of the Bible correct this error. "While the earth remaineth," so God is represented as assuring Noah,

MIRACLES AND SUPERNATURAL RELIGION

"seedtime and harvest, and cold and heat, and summer and winter, and day and night, shall not cease." The presence of God in his world was thus to be evinced by his regular sustaining of its natural order, rather than by irregular occurrences, such as the deluge, in seeming contravention of it. To seek the evidence of divine activity in human affairs and to ground one's faith in a controlling Providence in sporadic and cometary phenomena, rather than in the constant and cumulative signs of it to be seen in the majestic order of the starry skies, in the reign of intelligence throughout the cosmos, in the moral evolution of ancient savagery into modern philanthropy, in the historic manifestation throughout the centuries of a Power not our own that works for the increase of righteousness, is a mode of thought which in our time is being steadily and surely outgrown. It is one of those "idols of the tribe" whose power alike over civilized and uncivilized men is broken less by argument than by the ascent of man to wider horizons of knowledge.

It is for the gain of religion that it should be broken, of the spiritual religion whose God is not a tradition, a reminiscence, but a living presence, inhabiting alike the clod and the star, the flower in the crannied wall and the life of man. So thinking of God the religious man may rightly say, (Dr. Lyman *Abbott in The Outlook*, February) "If it is more difficult to believe in miracles, it is less important. If the extraordinary manifestations of God recounted in ancient history appear less credible, the ordinary manifestations of God in current life appear more real. He is seen in American history not less than in Hebrew history; in the life of today not less than in the life of long ago."

MIRACLES AND SUPERNATURAL RELIGION

SECTION II

SYNOPSIS: The present net results of the discussion of the miraculous element in the Bible. Evaporation of the former evidential value of miracles. Further insistence on this value a logical blunder. The transfer of miracles from the artillery to the baggage of the Church. Probability of a further reduction of the list of miracles. Also of a further transfer of events reputed miraculous to the domain of history.

The cultivation of scientific and historical studies during the last century, especially in its latter half, has deepened the conviction that "Through the ages one increasing purpose runs," disposed a growing number of thoughtful minds to regard occasional signs and wonders, reported from ancient times, as far less evidential for the reasonableness of religious faith than the steady sustaining of the Providential order and the moral progress of the world. Fully convinced of this, we should now estimate, before proceeding further, the present net results of the discussion, so far as it has gone, of what is called the miraculous element in the Bible.

First, its former evidential value in proof of divine Revelation is gone for the men of today. The believer in a divine Revelation does not now, if he is wise, rest his case at all on the miracles connected with its original promulgation, as was the fashion not very long since. This for two reasons; chiefly this: that the decisive criterion of any truth, ethical or physical, must be truth of the same kind. Ethical truth must be ethically attested. The moral and religious character of the Revelation presents its credentials of worth in its history of the moral and religious renovations it has wrought both in individuals and in society. This is its proper and incontrovertible attestation, in need of no corroboration from whatever wonderful physical

13

occurrences may have accompanied its first utterance. Words of God are attested as such by the work of God which they effect. It may well be believed that those wonderful occurrences the Biblical name for which is "signs," or "powers," terms not carrying, like "miracles," the idea of something contra-natural... (The Anglicized Latin word, "miracle," indiscriminately used in the Authorized Version, denotes the superficial character of the act or event it is applied to, as producing wonder or amazement in the beholders. The terms commonly employed in the New Testament (*semeion*, a sign; *dunamis*, power; less frequently *teras*, a portent) are of deeper significance, and connote the inner nature of the occurrence, either as requiring to be pondered for its meaning, or as the product of a new and peculiar energy.) ...had an evidential value for those to whom the Revelation originally came. In fact, they were appealed to by the bearers of the Revelation as evidencing its divine origin by the mighty works of divine mercy which they wrought for sufferers from the evils of the world. But whatever their evidential value to the eye-witnesses at that remote day, it was of the inevitably volatile kind that exhales away like a perfume with lapse of time. Historic doubts attack remote events, especially when of the extraordinary character which tempts the narrator to that magnifying of the marvelous which experience has found to be a constantly recurring human trait.

It is simply impossible that the original evidential value of the "signs" accompanying the Revelation should continue permanently unimpaired. To employ them now as "evidences of Christianity," when the Revelation has won on ethical grounds recognition of its divine character and can summon history to bear witness of its divine effects in the moral uplift of the world, is to imperil the Christian argument by the preposterous logical blunder of attempting to prove the more certain by the less certain. A second net result consequent on the preceding may be described as the transference of miracles from the ordnance department to the quartermaster's department of the Church. Until recently they were actively used as part of its armament, none of which could be dispensed with. Now they are carried as part of its baggage, impedimenta, from which everything superfluous must be removed.

It is clearly seen that to retain all is to imperil the whole. That there are miracles and miracles is patent to minds that have learned to scan history more critically than when a scholar like John Milton began his History of England with the legend of the voyage of "Brute the Trojan." One may reasonably believe that Jesus healed a case of violent insanity at Gadara, and reasonably disbelieve that the fire of heaven was twice obedient to Elijah's call to consume the military companies sent to arrest him. Cultivated discernment does not now put all Biblical miracles on a common level of credibility, any more than the historical work of Herodotus and that of the late Dr. Gardiner. To defend them all is not to vindicate, but to discredit all alike. The elimination of the indefensible, the setting aside of the legendary, the transference of the supposedly miraculous to the order of natural powers and processes so far as vindicable ground, for such critical treatment is discovered, is the only way to answer the first of all questions concerning the Bible: How much of this is credible history? Thus it is not only thoroughly reasonable, but is in the interest of a reasonable belief that divine agency is revealed rather by the upholding of the established order of Nature than by any alleged interference therewith. With what God has established God never interferes. To allege his interference with his established order is virtually to deny his constant immanence therein, a failure to recognize the fundamental fact that "Nature is Spirit," as Principal Fairbairn has said, and all its processes and powers the various modes of the energizing of the divine Will.

A third net result now highly probable is a still further

reduction of the list of reputed miracles. The critical process of discriminating the historical from the legendary, and the natural from the non-natural, is still so comparatively recent that it can hardly be supposed to have reached its limit. Nor can it be stayed by any impeachment of it as hostile to Christianity, whose grand argument appeals to its present ethical effects, not to ancient thaumaturgical accompaniments. There is, however, a considerable class of cases in which the advancing critical process is likely even to gain credibility for the Biblical narrative in a point where it is now widely doubted the resuscitation of the apparently dead. Among all the Biblical miracles none have more probably a secure historical basis.

MIRACLES AND SUPERNATURAL RELIGION

SECTION III

SYNOPSIS: Arbitrary criticism of the Biblical narratives of the raising of the "dead." Facts which it ignores. The subject related to the phenomena of trance, and records of premature burial. The resuscitation in Elisha's tomb probably historical. Jesus' raising of the ruler's daughter plainly a case of this kind. His raising of the widow's son probably such. The hypothesis that his raising of Lazarus may also have been such critically examined. The record allows this supposition. Further considerations favoring it: 1. The real interests of Christianity secure. 2. The miracle as a work of mercy. 3. Incompetency of the bystanders' opinion. 4. Congruity with the general conception of the healing works of Jesus, as wrought by a peculiar psychical power. Other cases. The resurrection of Jesus an event in a wholly different order of things. The practical result of regarding these resuscitations as in the order of nature.

If resuscitation from apparent death seven cases in all are recorded, three in the Old Testament and four in the New. Some critics arbitrarily reject all but one of these as legendary. Thus Oscar Holzmann, in his recent Leben Jesu, treats the raising of the widow's son, and of Lazarus. But he accepts the case of the ruler's daughter on the ground that Jesus is reported as saying that it was not a case of real but only of apparent death, "the child is not dead, but sleepeth." But for the preservation of this saving declaration in the record, this case also would have been classed with the others as unhistorical. And yet the admission of one clear case of simulated death, so like real death as to deceive all the onlookers but Jesus, might reasonably check the critic with the suggestion that it may not have been a solitary case. (An objection to the historicity of the raising of Lazarus which is made on the ground that so great a work, if historical, would have been related by more than one of the Evangelists,

17

yields on reflection the possibility that Jesus may have effected more than the three raisings recorded of him. John is the sole narrator of the raising of Lazarus. But he omits notice of the two raisings recorded by the other Evangelists, while Matthew and Mark do not record the raising of the widow's son recorded by Luke. All this suggests that the record may have preserved for us specimens rather than a complete list of this class of miracles. (Compare John xxi. 25.))

The headlong assumption involved in the discrimination made between these two classes, viz. that in a case of apparent but unreal death the primitive tradition can be depended on to put the fact upon record, is in the highest degree arbitrary and unwarrantable.

The skepticism which lightly contradicts the Biblical narratives of the raising of the "dead" to life is seemingly ignorant of facts that go far to place these upon firm ground as historical occurrences. Catalepsy, or the simulation of death by a trance, in which the body is sometimes cold and rigid, sensation gone, the heart still, is well known to medical men. ("We have frequent cases of trance... where the parties seem to die, but after a time the spirit returns, and life goes on as before. In all this there is no miracle. Why may not the resuscitations in Christ's time possibly have been similar cases? Is not this less improbable than that the natural order of the universe should have been set aside?" *The Problem of Final Destiny*, by William B. Brown, D.D., 1899.)

In early times such a condition would inevitably have been regarded and treated as actual death, without the least suspicion that it was not so. Even now, the dreadful mistake of so regarding it sometimes occurs. So cautious a journal as the London Spectator a few years ago expressed the belief that "a distinct percentage" of premature burials "occurs every year" in

MIRACLES AND SUPERNATURAL RELIGION

England.

The proper line of critical approach to the study of the Biblical narratives of the raising of the "dead" is through the well-known facts of the deathlike trance and premature burial. Where burial occurred, as in the East, immediately after the apparent death, (On account of the ceremonial "uncleanness" caused by the dead body. See Numbers v. 2, and many similar passages.) resuscitation must have been rare. Yet cases of it were not unknown. Pliny has a chapter "on those who have revived on being carried forth for burial." Lord Bacon states that of this there have been "very many cases." A French writer of the eighteenth century, Bruhier, in his *Dissertations sur l'Incertitude de la Mort et l'abus des Enterrements* records seventy-two cases of mistaken pronouncement of death, fifty-three of revival in the coffin before burial, and fifty-four of burial alive. A locally famous and thoroughly attested case in this country is that of the Rev. William Tennent, pastor in Freehold, New Jersey, in the eighteenth century, who lay apparently dead for three days, reviving from trance just as his delayed funeral was about to proceed. One who keeps a scrap-book could easily collect quite an assortment of such cases, and of such others as have a tragic ending, both from domestic and foreign journals. A work published some years ago by Dr. F. Hartmann (*Buried Alive* (Universal Truth Publishing Co., Chicago) . See also *Premature Burial*, by D. Walsh (William Wood & Co., New York), and *Premature Burial*, by W. Tebb and E. P. Vollum (New Amsterdam Book Co., New York).) exhibits one hundred and eight cases as typical among over seven hundred that have been authenticated. (Other writers might be mentioned, as Mme. Necker (1790), Dr. Vigm (1841). Yet on the other hand it is alleged, that "none of the numerous stories of this dreadful accident which have obtained credence from time to time seem to be authentic." (American Cyclopedia, art. "Burial"). Allowing a wide margin for exaggeration and credulity, there is certainly a residuum of fact. A correspondent of the (London) Spectator a few years since testified to a distressing case in his own family.

Facts like these have been strangely overlooked in the hasty judgment prompted by prejudice against whatever has obtained credence as miraculous. Some significant considerations must be seriously entertained. It cannot be that no such facts occurred in the long periods covered by the Biblical writers. Occurring, it is extremely improbable that they should have altogether escaped embodiment in popular tradition and its record. Furthermore, while on one hand the custom of speedy burial rendered them much rarer than they are now under other conditions, and so much the more extraordinary, the universal ignorance of the causes involved would have accepted resuscitation as veritable restoration from actual death. As such it would have passed into tradition. In cases where it had come to pass in connection with the efforts of a recognized prophet, or through any contact with him, it would certainly have been regarded as a genuine miracle.

Among the raisings of the "dead" recorded in the Scriptures probably none has been so widely doubted by critical readers as the story in the thirteenth chapter of the second book of Kings, in which a corpse is restored to life by contact with the bones of Elisha. Dean Stanley's remark upon the suspicious similarity between the miracles related of Elisha and those found in Roman Catholic legends of great saints here seems quite pertinent. Let the record speak for itself.

"And Elisha died and they buried him. Now the bands of the Moabites invaded the land at the coming in of the year. And it came to pass, as they were burying a man, that, behold, they spied a band; and they cast the man into the sepulcher of Elisha, and as soon as the man touched the bones of Elisha, he revived, and stood up on his feet."

MIRACLES AND SUPERNATURAL RELIGION

The bizarre character of such a story excusably predisposes many a critic to stamp it as fabricated to enhance the glory of the great prophet who had been a pillar of the throne. Yet nothing is more likely than that tradition has here preserved a bit of history, extraordinary, but real. There is not the least improbability in regarding the case as one of the many revivals from the deathlike trance that have been noted by writers ancient and modern. It is entirely reasonable to suppose that the trance in which the seemingly dead man lay was broken either by the shock of his fall into the prophet's tomb, or coincidentally therewith; and stranger coincidences have happened.

Such a happening would be precisely the sort of thing to live in popular tradition, and to be incorporated into the annals of the time. Here it may be rejoined that this is only a hypothesis. Only that, to be sure. But so is the allegation that the story is a mere fantastic fabrication only a hypothesis. Demonstration of the actual fact past all controversy being out of the question, all that can be offered for the attempt to rate the narrative at its proper value, either as history or as fiction, is hypothesis. The choice lies for us between two hypotheses. Surely, that hypothesis is the more credible which is based on a solid body of objective facts, and meets all the conditions of the case.

Will it be replied to this that the critics can show for their hypothesis the admitted fact of the human proclivity to invent legends of miracle? The decisive answer is that the burden of proof rests on him who contests any statement ostensibly historical. If such a statement be found to square with admitted objective facts, it must be accepted notwithstanding considerations drawn from the subjective tendency to invent extraordinary tales. Were raisings of the "dead" recorded in the Old Testament alone, objection would less often be offered to this transference of them, along with other occurrences once deemed miraculous, to a place in the natural order of things. The statistics of premature burial and of the resuscitation of the apparently dead before burial are sufficiently strong to throw grave doubt on any contention that the resuscitations narrated of Elijah (1 Kings xvii. 17-23.) and Elisha (1 Kings iv. 32-36.) do not belong in that historical series. It has been frequently observed, however, that there is much reluctance to apply to the New Testament the methods and canons of criticism that are applied to the Old. It will be so in the present case, through apprehension of somehow detracting from the distinctive glory of Christ. That fear will not disturb one who sees that glory not in his "mighty works," the like of which were wrought by the prophets, but in the spiritual majesty of his personality, the divinity of his message to the world, and of the life and death that illustrated it.

One case, at least, among Jesus' raisings of the "dead," that of the young daughter of the ruler of the synagogue (2 Mark v. 35-43.) is admitted even by skeptical critics to have been a resuscitation from the trance that merely simulates death. But the fact that there is a record of his saying in this case, "the child is not dead, but sleepeth," and no record of his saying the same at the bier of the widow's son, (Luke vii. 12-16.) is slight ground, yet all the ground there is, against the great probabilities to the contrary, for regarding the latter case as so transcendentally different from the former as the actual re-embodiment of a departed spirit recalled from another world. Were these the only two cases of restoration to life in the ministry of Jesus, it is most probable that they would be regarded as of the same kind. The raising of Lazarus (John xi. 1 1-44.) presents peculiar features, in view of which it is generally regarded as of another kind, and the greatest of miracles, so stupendous that the Rev. W. J. Dawson, in his recent *Life of Christ*, written from an evangelical standpoint, says of it; "Even the most devout mind may be forgiven occasional pangs of incredulity." But the considerations already presented are certainly sufficient to justify a reexamination of the case. And it is to be borne in mind that the question at issue is, not what the eye-witnesses at that time believed, not what the Church from that time to this has believed, not what we are willing to believe, or would like to believe, but what all the facts with any bearing on the case, taken together, fully justify us in believing as to the real nature of it.

What Jesus is recorded as saying of it is, of course, of prime importance. "Our friend Lazarus is fallen asleep, but I go that I may awake him out of sleep." Were this all, the case might easily have been classed as one of trance. The disciples, however, understood Jesus to speak of natural sleep. "Then Jesus therefore said unto them plainly, Lazarus is dead." Tradition puts the maximum meaning into this word "dead." But if this word here qualifies the preceding word, "fallen asleep," so also is it qualified by that; the two are mutually explanatory, not contradictory. These alternatives are before us: Is the maximum or the minimum meaning to be assigned to the crucial word "dead"? For the minimum, one can say that a deathly trance, already made virtual death by immediate interment, would amply justify Jesus in using the word "dead" in order to impress the disciples with the gravity of the case, as not a natural but a deathly, and, in the existing situation, a fatal sleep. For the maximum, no more can be advanced than the hazardous assertion that Jesus must have used the word with technical precision in its customary sense; an assertion of course protected from disproof by our ignorance of the actual fact. (Was Jesus aware that Lazarus was really not dead? It is impossible to reach a positive conclusion. In some directions his knowledge was certainly limited. That he was not aware of the reality might be inferred from his seeming to have allowed his act to pass for what, in the view of it here suggested, it was not, the recall to life of one actually dead. This, however, assumes the completeness of a record whose silence on this point cannot be pressed as conclusive. It is, indeed, unlikely that Jesus knew all that

23

medical men now know. But awareness of any fact may be in varying degrees from serious suspicion up to positive certitude. While far from positiveness, awareness may exist in a degree that gives courage for resolute effort resulting in clear and full verification. Jesus may have been ignorant of the objective reality of Lazarus's condition, and yet have been very hopeful of being empowered by the divine aid he prayed for (John xi. 41) to cope with it successfully.) But whatever support this view of the case derives from such ignorance is overbalanced by the support supplied to the other view by the long history of revivals from the deathly trance, and by the probabilities which that history creates.

Many, to whom the view here proposed seems not only new, but unwelcome, and even revolutionary, may reasonably prefer to suspend judgment for reflection; but meanwhile some further considerations may be entertained:

1. Aside from the unwillingness to abandon a long-cherished belief on any subject whatever, which is both a natural, and, when not pushed to an unreasonable length, a desirable brake on all inconsiderate change, no practical interest is threatened by the adoption of the view here suggested. Religious interest, so far as it is also intelligent, is certainly not threatened. The evidences of Jesus' divine character and mission resting, as for modern men it rests, not on remote wonders, but on now acknowledged facts of an ethical and spiritual kind, is altogether independent of our conclusion whether it was from actual or only apparent death that Lazarus was raised. Since all the mighty works wrought by Jesus, and this among them, were identical in type with those wrought by the ancient prophets, with whom his countrymen classed him in his lifetime, their evidential significance could be, even for the eye-witnesses at that tomb, no greater for him than for an Elisha, signs of a divine mission attesting itself by works of mercy.

MIRACLES AND SUPERNATURAL RELIGION

2. As works of mercy these raisings from the "dead," including that of Lazarus, rank far higher in the view of them here proposed than in the traditional view. This regards them as the recall of departed spirits from what is hoped to be "a better world." Yet this, while it turns sorrow for a time into joy, involves not only the recurrence of that sorrow in all its keenness, but also a second tasting of the pains preliminary to the death-gate, when the time comes to pass that gate again. But in the other view, a raising from the death that is only simulated is a merciful deliverance from a calamity greater than simple death, if that be any calamity at all, the fate of burial alive. In the former view, therefore, the quality of mercy, distinctive of the mighty works of Jesus, is imperfectly demonstrable. In the present view, as the rescue of the living from death in one of its most horrible forms, it is abundantly conspicuous.

3. The onlookers by the tomb of Lazarus doubtless regarded his awakening as revival from actual death. Their opinion, however, does not bind our judgment any more than it is bound by the opinion of other onlookers, that Jesus' healing of the insane and epileptic was through the expulsion of demons that possessed them. In each instance it was understood as a sign of control over beings belonging to another world. But such an attestation of Jesus' divine mission, having been superseded for us by proofs of higher character, is now no more needful for us in the case of the "dead" than in the case of the "demons."

4. The power of breaking the deathly trance, of quickening the dormant life, re-energizing the collapsed nervous organism, and ending its paralysis of sensation and motion, may be reasonably regarded as power of the same psychical kind that Jesus regularly exerted in healing the sufferers from nervous disorders who were reputed victims of demoniac possession. In this view these resuscitations from apparent death appear in natural coherence with the many other works of mercy that Jesus

25

wrought as the Great Physician of his people, and may be regarded as the crown and consummation of all his restorative ministries.

Jesus' thanksgiving after the tomb had been opened "Father, I thank thee that thou hast heard me" shows that he had girded himself for a supreme effort by concentrating the utmost energy of his spirit in prayer. Physically parallel with this was the intensity of voice put into his call to the occupant of the tomb. This is better represented in the original than in our translation: "He shouted with a great voice, 'Lazarus, come forth.'" The whole record indicates the utmost tension of all his energies, and closely comports with the view that this stood to the sequel in the relation of cause to effect. (Jesus' works of healing are explicitly attributed by the Evangelists to a peculiar power that issued from him. In Mark v. 30, Luke vi. 19, and viii. 46, the original word dunamis, which the Authorized Version translates "virtue," is more correctly rendered "power" in the Revised Version. Especially noticeable is the peculiar phraseology of Mark v. 30: "Jesus perceiving in himself that the power proceeding from him had gone forth (R. V.)." The peculiar circumstances of the case suggest that the going forth of this power might be motivated sub-consciously, as well as by conscious volition.)

Another circumstance not without bearing on the case is the energizing power of the intense sympathy with the bereaved family that stirred the soul of Jesus to weep and groan with them. And it is not without significance that this strong factor appears active in the larger number of the Biblical cases, three of them only children, two of these the children of the pitiable class of widows.

Peculiar, then, as was the case of Lazarus, our examination of it reveals no substantial ground for insisting that it was essentially unlike the previous case of the ruler's daughter, that it was the bringing back into a decaying body of a spirit that had entered into the world of departed souls. The actual fact, of course, is indemonstrable. Our conclusion has to be formed wholly upon the probabilities of the case, and must be formed in a reasonable choice between the greater probability and the less.

The restoration of Dorcas to life by Peter, recorded in the book of Acts, (Acts ix. 36-42.) needs no special discussion beyond the various considerations already adduced in this chapter. The case of Eutychus, recorded in the same book, (Acts xx. 9-13.) requires mention only lest it should seem to have been forgotten, as it is not in point at all. The record makes it highly probable that the supposed death was nothing more than the loss of consciousness for a few hours in consequence of a fall from the window.

If one should here suggest that no mention has yet been made of the resurrection of Jesus himself, it must be pointed out that this is a fact of a totally different kind from any of the foregoing cases. To speak, as many do, of the "resurrection of Lazarus" is a misuse of words. Resuscitation to life in this world, and resurrection, the rising up of the released spirit into the life of the world to come, are as distinct as are the worlds to which they severally belong. We here consider only the raisings which restored to the virtually dead their interrupted mortal life. The rising from the mortal into the immortal state belongs to an entirely different field of study.

Apart, then, from traditional prepossessions, examination of the Biblical narratives discloses nothing to invalidate the hypothesis which one who is acquainted with the copious record of apparent but unreal death must seriously and impartially consider. The reputedly miraculous raisings of the "dead" related in both the Old and the New Testament may, with entire reason, and without detriment to religion, be classed with such as are related outside of the Scriptures, in ancient times as well as modern, and as phenomena wholly within the natural order, however extraordinary.

The practical result of such a conclusion is likely to be a gain for the historicity of the Scripture narratives in the estimate of a large class of thoughtful minds.

MIRACLES AND SUPERNATURAL RELIGION

SECTION IV

SYNOPSIS: A clearer conception of miracle approached. Works of Jesus once reputed miraculous not so reputed now, since not now transcending, as once, the existing range of knowledge and power. This transfer of the miraculous to the natural likely to continue. No hard and fast line between the miraculous and the non-miraculous. Miracle a provisional word, its application narrowing in the enlarging mastery of the secrets of nature and life.

At this point it seems possible to approach a clearer understanding of the proper meaning to attach to the generally ill-defined and hazy term miracle. ("Early and medieval theologians agree in conceiving the miraculous as being above, not contrary to, nature. The question entered on a new phase when Hume defined a miracle as a violation of nature, and asserted the impossibility of substantiating its actual occurrence. The modern discussion has proceeded largely in view of Hume's destructive criticism. Assuming the possibility of a miracle, the questions of fact and of definition remain." *Dictionary of Psychology.* "When we find the definition for which we are searching, the miraculous will no longer be a problem." Professor W. Sanday, at the Anglican Church Congress, 1902.)

Matthew Arnold's fantastic illustration of the idea of miracle by supposing a pen changed to a pen-wiper may fit some miracles, especially those of the Catholic hagiology, but, if applied to those of Jesus, would be a caricature. In the New Testament a reputed miracle is not any sort of wonderful work upon any sort of occasion, but an act of benevolent will exerted for an immediate benefit, (For exceptions see Matthew xxi. 19; Acts xiii. 10, ii.) and transcending the then existing range of human intelligence to explain and power to achieve. The historic reality of at least some such acts performed by Jesus is acknowledged by critics as free from the faintest trace of orthodox bias as Keim: "The picture of Jesus, the worker of miracles, belongs to the first believers in Christ, and is no invention."

It has already been noted that a considerable number of the then reputed miracles of Jesus, particularly his works of healing, do not now, as then, transcend the existing range of knowledge and power, and accordingly are no longer reputed miraculous. And one cannot reasonably believe that a limit to the understanding and control of forces in Nature and mind that now are more or less occult has been already reached. It is, therefore, not incredible that some of the mighty works of Jesus, which still transcend the existing limits of knowledge and power, and so are still reputed miraculous, and are suspected by many as unhistorical, may in some yet remote and riper stage of humanity be transferred, as some have already been, to the class of the non-miraculous and natural.

Dr. Robbins, Dean of the General Theological Seminary, New York, after remarking that "the word miracle has done more to introduce confusion into Christian Evidences than any other," goes on to say: "To animals certain events to them inexplicable are signs of the presence of human intelligence and power. To men these miracles of Christ are signs of divine intelligence and power. But how is miracle to be differentiated from other providential dealings of God? Not by removing him further from common events. Abstruse speculations concerning the relation of miracles to other physical phenomena may be safely left to the adjustment of an age which shall have advanced to a more perfect synthesis of knowledge than the present can boast." (*A Christian Apologetic* p. 97.)

The truth to which such considerations conduct is, that

no hard and fast line can be drawn between the miraculous and the non-miraculous. To the untutored mind, like that of the savage who thought it miraculous that a chip with a message written on it had talked to the recipient, the simplest thing that he cannot explain is miraculous: "*omne ignotnm pro mirifico*" said Tacitus. As the range of knowledge and power widens, the range of the miraculous narrows correspondingly. Some twenty years since, the International Sunday-school Lessons employed as a proof of the divinity of Christ the reputedly miraculous knowledge which he evinced in his first interview with Nathanael of a solitary hour in Nathanael's experience. (John i. 47-50.)

Since then it has been demonstrated (In the opinion of such psychologists as Professor William James, of Harvard, the late Professor Henry Sidgwick, of Cambridge, England, and others of like eminence.) by psychical research that the natural order of the world includes telepathy, and the range of the miraculous has been correspondingly reduced without detriment to the argument for the divinity of Christ, now rested on less precarious ground.

Under such conditions as we have reviewed a miracle cannot always be one and the same thing. Miracle must therefore be defined as being what our whole course of thought has suggested that it is; in general, an elastic word, in particular, a provisional word, a word whose application narrows with the enlarging range of human knowledge (A hint of this was given by Augustine: "*Portentum non fit contra naturam, sed contra quam est nota natura.*" *De Civitate Dei*.) and power which for the time it transcends; a word whose history, in its record of ranges already transcended, prompts expectation that ranges still beyond may be transcended in the illimitable progress of mankind.

MIRACLES AND SUPERNATURAL RELIGION

Professor Le Conte says that miracle is "an occurrence or a phenomenon according to a law higher than any yet known." Thus it is a case of human ignorance, not of divine interference. On the other hand, we must believe that the goal of progress is a flying goal; that human attainment can never reach finality unless men cease to be. And so all widening of human knowledge and power must ever disclose further limitations to be transcended. There will always be a Beyond, in which dwells the secret of laws still undiscovered, that underlie mysteries unrevealed and marvels unexplained. This will have to be admitted, especially, by those to whom the marvelous is synonymous with the incredible. We have not been able to eviscerate even these prosaic and matter-of-fact modern times of marvels whose secret lies in the yet uncatalogued or indefinable powers of the mysterious agent that we name life: witness many well verified facts recorded by the Society for Psychical Research. (Consult the late F. W. H. Myers's remarkable volumes on *Human Personality and Survival after Death* (Longmans, Green & Co).)

How, then, is it consistent to affirm that no such marvels in ancient records are historical realities? Nay, may it not be true that the ancient days of seers and prophets, the days of Jesus, days of the sublime strivings of great and lonely souls for closer converse with the Infinite Spirit behind his mask of Nature, offered better conditions for marvelous experiences and deeds than these days of scientific laboratories and factories, and world-markets and world-politics?

MIRACLES AND SUPERNATURAL RELIGION

SECTION V

SYNOPSIS. Biblical miracles the effluence of extraordinary lives. Life the world's magician and miracle worker; its miracles now termed prodigies. Miracle the natural product of an extraordinary endowment of life. Life the ultimate reality. What any man can achieve is conditioned by the psychical quality of his life. Nothing more natural, more supernatural, than life. The derived life of the world filial to the self-existent life of God, "begotten, not made." Miracle, as the product of life, the work of God.

Be it noted, now, that the marvelous phenomena of the Biblical record, whatever else be thought of them, are, even to a superficial view, the extraordinary effluence of extraordinary lives. Here at length we gain a clearer conception of miracle. Life is the world's great magician, life, so familiar, yet so mysterious; so commonplace, yet so transcendent No miracle is more marvelous than its doings witnessed in the biological laboratory, or more inexplicable than its transformation of dead matter into living flesh, its development of a Shakespeare from a microscopic bit of protoplasm.

But its mysterious processes are too common for general marvel; we marvel only at the uncommon. The boy Zerah Colburn in half a minute solved the problem, "How many seconds since the beginning of the Christian era?" We prefer to call this a prodigy rather than a miracle, a distinction more verbal than real; and we fancy we have explained it when we say that such arithmetical power was a peculiar endowment of his mental life. Now all of the inexplicable, inimitable reality that at any time has to be left by the baffled intellect as an unsolved wonder under the name of miracle is just that, the natural product of an extraordinary endowment of life. More of its marvelous capability is latent in common men, in the subconscious depths of being, than has ever yet flashed forth in the career of uncommon men. Some scientists say that it depends on chemical and physical forces. It indeed uses these to build the various bodies it inhabits, but again it leaves these to destroy those bodies when it quits them. The most constant and ubiquitous phenomenon in the world, the ultimate reality in the universe, is life, revealing its presence in innumerable modes of activity, from the dance of atoms in the rock to the philosophizing of the sage and the aspirations of the saint, the creator of Nature, the administrator of the regular processes we call the laws of Nature, the author of the wonders men call miraculous because they are uncommon and ill understood.

The works of which any man is naturally capable are conditioned by the psychical quality of his life, and its power to use the forces of Nature. Through differences of vital endowment some can use color, as wonderful painters, and others employ sound, as wonderful musicians, in ways impossible to those otherwise endowed. So "a poet is born, not made." So persons of feeble frame, stimulated by disease or frenzied by passion, have put forth preternatural and prodigious muscular strength. By what we call "clairvoyant" power life calls up in intelligent perception things going on far beyond ocular vision. By what we call "telepathic" power life communicates intelligence with life separated by miles of space. Such are some of the powers that have been discovered, and fully attested, but not explained, as belonging to the world's master magician, Life. And when the poet asks, "Ah, what will our children be, The men of a hundred thousand, a million summers away?" we can only answer with the Apostle: "It doth not yet appear what we shall be."

But we cannot deem it likely that the powers of life, "Deep seated in our mystic frame," and giving forth such flashes of their inherent virtue, have already reached their ultimate development.

We look with wonder and awe into the secret shrine of life, where two scarcely visible cells unite to form the human being whose thought shall arrange the starry heavens in majestic order, and harness the titanic energies of Nature for the world's work. There we behold the real supernatural. (Nothing is more natural than life, and nothing also more supernatural.) Biology studies all the various forms that the world shows of it, and affirms that life, though multiform, is one.

This embryology attests, showing that the whole ascent of life through diverse forms from the lowest to the highest, during the millions of years since life first manifested its presence on this globe, is recapitulated in the stages of growth through which the human being passes in the few months before its birth. And philosophy, which does not seek the living among the dead, affirms, *omne vivum ex vivo*. The varied but unitary life of the world is the stream of an inexhaustible spring. It is filial to the life of God, the Father Almighty. What the ancient creed affirmed of the Christ as the Son of God whom his beloved disciple recognized as "the eternal life which was with the Father and was manifested unto us" (i John i. 2) may be truly affirmed of the mysterious reality that is known as life: "Begotten not made, being of one substance with the Father; through whom (or which) all things were made."

Looking from the derived and finite life of the world, visible only in the signs of its presence, but in its reality no more visible than him "whom no man hath seen, nor can see" up to the life underived, aboriginal, infinite, we recognize God and Life as terms of identical significance. How superficial the notion of miracles as "the personal intervention of God into the chain of cause and effect," in which he is the constant vital element. If an event deemed miraculous is ever ascribed, as of old, to "the finger of God," the reality behind the phenomenon is simply a higher or a stronger power of life than is recognized in an event of a common type life that is one with the infinite and universal Life:

> "Life that in me has rest,
> As I, undying Life, have power in Thee."

MIRACLES AND SUPERNATURAL RELIGION

SECTION VI

SYNOPSIS. The question, both old and new, now confronting theologians. Their recent retreat upon the minimum of miracle. The present conflict of opinion in the Church. Its turning-point reached in the antipodal turn-about in the treatment of miracles from the old to the new apologetics. Revision of the traditional idea of the supernatural required for theological readjustment.

The present line of thought has now reached the point where an important question confronts us, a question not wholly new. Within the memory of living men theologians have been compelled to ask themselves: What if the geologists should establish facts that contradict our Biblically derived doctrine that the universe was made in a week? Again have they been constrained to put to themselves the question: What if the evolutionists should supersede our doctrine that the creation is the immediate product of successive fiats of the Creator by showing that it came gradually into existence through the progressive operation of forces immanent in the cosmos? Still again have they had to face the question: What if modern criticism by the discovery of demonstrable errors in the Sacred Writings should fault our doctrine that, as the Word of God, the Bible is free from all and every error? In every instance the dreaded concession, when found at length to be enforced by modern learning, has been found to bring, not the loss that had been apprehended, but clear gain to the intellectual interests of religion. Now it is this same sort of question which returns with the uncertainties and difficulties widely felt in the Church to be gathering over its hitherto unvexed belief in miracles as signs of a divine activity more immediate than it has recognized in the regular processes of Nature.

MIRACLES AND SUPERNATURAL RELIGION

The majority of uneducated Christians still hold, as formerly in each of the points just mentioned, to the traditional view. Miracle as a divine intervention in the natural order, a more close and direct divine contact with the course of things than is the case in ordinary experience, they regard as the inseparable and necessary concomitant and proof of a divine Revelation. To deny miracles, thus understood, is censured as equivalent to denial of the reality of the Revelation.

But it is rather surprising, because it is rare, to find a man of such note in literature as Dr. W. Robertson Nicoll affirming... ("The Church asks, and it is entitled to ask the critic: Do you believe in the Incarnation and Resurrection of Jesus Christ?... If he replies in the negative, he has missed the way, and has put himself outside of the Church of Christ." The Church's One Foundation, p. 4. (Note that "Incarnation" and "Resurrection" are terms which Dr. Nicoll construes as denoting physical miracles.) What Dr. Nicoll here means by "outside of the Church" he indicates by saying elsewhere, that philosophers who reckon goodness as everything, and miracles as impossible, "are not Christians." (op. cit., p. 10). This conditioning of Christian character upon an intellectual judgment concerning the reality of remote occurrences is both unbiblical and unethical, as well as absurd when practically applied. Some years since, Dr. E. A. Abbott, who admits no miracle in the life of Christ, published a book, The Spirit on the Waters, in which he inculcated the worship of Christ. Yet, according to Dr. Nicoll, such a man is no Christian!) ...that one cannot be a Christian without believing at least two miracles, the virgin birth and the physical resurrection of the Christ. Without comment on the significance of this retreat upon the minimum of miracle, it must here be noted that a minority of the Church, not inferior to their brethren in learning and piety, believe that there are no tides in God's presence in Nature, that his contact with it is always of the closest: "Closer is he than breathing, and nearer than hands or feet."

MIRACLES AND SUPERNATURAL RELIGION

All natural operations are to them divine operations. "Nature," said Dr. Martineau, "is God's mask, not his competitor." While his agency in Nature may be recognized at one time more than at another, it exists at any time fully as much as at any other. In the interest of this fundamental truth of religion they affirm that miracles in the traditional sense of the word, and in their traditional limitation to the small measure of time and space covered by Biblical narratives, never occurred. Events reputed miraculous have indeed occurred, but simply as unusual, inexplicable phenomena in the natural order of things, the natural products of exceptionally endowed life, and, whether in ancient time or modern, the same sort of thing the world over.

To the argument that this involves denial of a supernatural Revelation they reply that it is mere reasoning in a circle. For if one begs the question at the outset by defining supernatural Revelation as revelation necessarily evidenced by miraculous divine intervention, then, of course, denial of this is denial of that, and how is the argument advanced? But, besides this, the question-begging definition is a fallacious confusing of the contents of the Revelation with its concomitants, and of its essentially spiritual character with phenomena in the sphere of the senses. The turning-point in this argument between the two parties in the Church has been reached in the antipodal change, already referred to, from the old to the new apologetics, a change whose inevitable consequences do not yet seem to be clearly discerned by either party in the discussion. The contention that denial of miracles as traditionally understood carries denial of supernatural Revelation has been virtually set aside, with its question- begging definition and circular reasoning, by the apologetics now current among believers in at least a minimum of miracle in the traditional sense of the word, especially in the two chief miracles of the virgin birth and the physical resurrection of Jesus. As an eminent representative of these the late Dr. A. B. Bruce may be cited. These adduce "the moral miracle," the sinlessness of Jesus, as evidential for the reality of the physical miracles as its "congruous accompaniments.", "If," says Dr. Bruce, "we receive Him as the great moral miracle, we shall receive much more for His sake." (*The Miraculous Element in the Gospels*, p. 353.) But what a turn-about of the traditional argument on the evidences!

The older apologetes argued: This crown of miraculous power bespeaks the royal dignity of the wearer. The modern apologete reasons: This royal character must have a crown of miraculous power corresponding with his moral worth. In this antipodal reverse of Christian thought it is quite plain that for evidential purposes the miracle is stripped of its ancient value. And it has already been observed that modern knowledge has now transferred many of the Biblical miracles to the new rooms discovered for them in the natural order of things. It is not premature, therefore, for leaders of Christian thought to put once more to themselves the question, constantly recurring as learning advances: What theological readjustment should we have to make, if obliged to concede that the ancient belief in miracle is not inseparable from belief in a supernatural Revelation, not indispensable to belief therein? What modified conception must we form, if constrained to admit that the living God, ever immanent in Nature, intervenes in Nature no more at one time than another? What, indeed, but a revised and true in place of a mistaken conception of the term Supernatural?

MIRACLES AND SUPERNATURAL RELIGION

SECTION VII

SYNOPSIS: Account to be made of the law of atrophy through disuse. The virgin birth and the corporeal resurrection of Jesus, the two miracles now insisted on as the irreducible minimum, affected by this law. The vital truths of the incarnation and immortality independent of these miracles. These truths now placed on higher ground in a truer conception of the supernatural. The true supernatural is. the spiritual, not the miraculous. Skepticism bred from the contrary view. The miracle narratives, while less evidential for religion, not unimportant for history. Psychical research a needful auxiliary for the scientific critic of these.

To the true conception of the supernatural we shall presently come. But we cannot proceed without briefly reminding ourselves of the certain consequences of this now far advanced dropping of miracles by modern apologetics from their ancient use as evidences of a supernatural Revelation. We are not ignorant of the law, which holds throughout the material, the mental, and the moral realms, that disuse tends to atrophy and extinction. Disused organs cease to exist, as in the eyeless cave-fish. For centuries the story of the miraculous birth of Jesus was serviceable for confirmation of his claim to be the Son of God. In the address of the angel of the annunciation to Mary that claim is expressly rested on the miraculous conception of "the holy thing." (Luke i. 35.) But as ethical enlightenment grows, the conviction grows that, whether the physiological ground of that claim be tenable or not, the ethical ground of it is essentially higher. Father and son even in human relationships are terms of more than physiological import. It is matter of frequent experience that, where the ethical character of such relationship is lacking, the physiological counts for nothing. Moreover, the divine sonship of Jesus in a purely ethical view rests on ground

41

not only higher but incontestable. And so in our time theologians prefer to rest it on foundations that cannot be shaken, on his moral oneness with God, the divinity of his spirit, the ideal perfectness of his life. The strength of this position being realized, the world begins to hear from Christian thinkers the innovating affirmation that belief of the miraculous birth can no longer be deemed essential to Christianity; else it would not have been left unmentioned in two of the four Gospels, and in every extant Apostolic letter. And now we hear theologians saying:

"I accept it, but I place it no more among the evidences of Christianity. I defend it, but cannot employ it in the defense of supernatural Revelation." Such a stage of thought is only transitional. An antiquated argument does not long survive in the world of thought. (To what extent the law of atrophy has begun to work upon the doctrine of the virgin birth appears in the recent utterance of so eminent an evangelical scholar as Dr. R. F. Horton, of London. The following report of his remarks in a Christmas sermon in 1901 is taken from the Christian World, London. "We could not imagine Paul, Peter, and John all ignoring something essential to the Gospel they preached. Strictly speaking, this narrative in Matthew and Luke was one of the latest touches in the Gospel, belonging to a period forty or fifty years after the Lord had passed away, when men had begun to realize what he was the Son of God and tried to express their conviction in this form or that." The implication here is unmistakable, that, in Dr. Horton's view, subjective considerations in the minds of pious believers, rather than objective fact, form the basis of the story.)

Military weapons that have become unserviceable soon find their way either to the museum or the foundry. It is shortsighted not to foresee the inevitable effect on our theological material of the law of atrophy through disuse. The case of the miracle is the case of a pillar originally put in for the support of an ancient roof. When the roof has a modern truss put beneath it springing from wall to wall, the pillar becomes an obstacle, and is removed. But as in such a case the roof, otherwise supported, does not fall in when the pillar is removed, so neither is the central Christian truth of the incarnation imperiled by any weakening or vanishing of belief in the doctrine of the virgin birth. In a discussion of the subject in Convocation at York, England, while these pages were being written, the Dean of Ripon (Dr. Boyd Carpenter) urged that it must be borne in mind that the incarnation and the virgin birth were two different things, and that some who found difficulty in the latter fully accepted the former. In a recent sermon Dr. Briggs insists likewise upon this: "The virgin birth is only one of many statements of the mode of incarnation... The doctrine of the incarnation does not depend upon the virgin birth... It is only a minor matter connected with the incarnation, and should have a subordinate place in the doctrine... At the same time the virgin birth is a New Testament doctrine, and we must give it its proper place and importance... The favorite idea of the incarnation among the people has ever been the simpler one of the virgin birth, as in the Ave Maria. The theologians have ever preferred the more profound doctrine of the Hymn of the Logos (John i. 1-18.)" (See the Sermon on "Born of a Virgin," in the volume on *The Incarnation of Our Lord*.)

Nay, it may even be found that the weakening of belief in the incarnation as an isolated and miraculous event may tend to promote a profounder conception of it, that brings the divine and the human into touch and union at all points instead of in one point. ("Christian thought has not erred by asserting too much concerning the incarnation of God, but, on the contrary, too little... If ever overblown by blasts of denial, it is for wanting breadth of base... Men have disbelieved the incarnation, because told that all there was of it was in Christ; and they reject what is presented as exceptional to the general way of God. They must be told to believe more; that the age-long way of God is in a perpetually increasing incarnation of life, whose climax and crown is the divine fullness of life in Christ." From a discourse by the present writer on "Life and its Incarnations," in the volume, *New Points to Old Texts*. (James Clarke & Co., London. Thomas Whittaker, New York, 1889.)

A similar change of thought, less remarked than its significance deserves, is concerned with that other great miracle, the corporeal resurrection of Jesus, which such writers as Dr. Nicoll couple with that of his virgin birth as the irreducible minimum of miracle, belief in which is essential to Christian discipleship. For many centuries the resurrection story in the Gospels has served as the conclusive proof both of the divine sonship of Jesus, (Romans, i. 4.) and of our own resurrection to immortality. (I Corinthians, xv. 16-23.) In the churches it is still popularly regarded as the supreme, sufficient, and indispensable fact required for the basis of faith. But in many a Christian mind the thought has dawned, that a single fact cannot give adequate ground for the general inference of a universal principle; that a remote historical fact, however strongly attested, can evince only what has taken place in a given case, not what will or must occur in other cases; while it is also inevitably more or less pursued by critical doubt of the attestations supporting it.

This rising tide of reflection has compelled resort to higher ground, to the inward evidences in the nature of mind that are more secure from the doubt to which all that is merely external and historical is exposed. A clear distinction has been discerned between the real resurrection of Jesus his rising from the mortal state into the immortal, and his phenomenal resurrection the manifestations of his change that are related as having been objectively witnessed. What took place in the invisible world his real resurrection is now more emphasized by Christian thinkers than the phenomenal resurrection in the visible world. So conservatively orthodox a writer as Dr. G. D. Boardman goes so far as to say: "After all, the real question in the matter of his resurrection is not, 'Did Christ's body rise?' That is but a subordinate, incidental issue."

The real question, as Dr. Boardman admits, is, "Whether Jesus Christ himself is risen, and is alive to-day." (*Our Risen King's Forty Days*, 1902.) The main stress of Christian thought today is not laid, as formerly, on the phenomena recorded in the story of the resurrection, but on the psychological, moral, and rational evidences of a resurrection to immortality that until recent times were comparatively disregarded. (In strong contrast with this are the reactionary protests of Dr. W. R. Nicoll: "To talk of the resurrection of the spirit is preposterous. The spirit does not die, and therefore cannot rise. The one resurrection of which the New Testament knows, the one resurrection which allows to language any meaning, is the resurrection of the body, the resurrection which leaves the grave empty." (op. Cit. p. 134). It should be noted here that Jesus' argument with the Sadducees on the resurrection (Luke xx. 37, 38) logically proceeds on the assumption that living after death and rising after death are convertible terms. Also, that the contrast involved in the idea of the resurrection (the anastasis, or rising up) is a contrast not between the grave and the sky, but between the lower life of mortals and the higher life immortal." For an extended exhibition of this line of evidence see "*The Assurance of Immortality,*" and "*The Present Pledge of Life to Come*" (in two volumes of discourses by the present writer), London, James Clarke & Co. New York, Thomas Whittaker, 1888 and 1889.) Meanwhile the vindication of the reality of the phenomena related of the risen Jesus, including his bodily ascension, though not a matter of indifference to many of those who have found the higher grounds of faith, has become to them of subordinate importance.

It is well for Christian faith that its super-sensuous and

impregnable grounds have been occupied. It is certain that ancient records of external phenomena cannot in future constitute, as heretofore, the stronghold of faith. But it is by no means yet certain that they have lost serviceableness as, at least, outworks of the stronghold. While the doctrine of the virgin birth seems to be threatened by atrophy, the doctrine of the bodily resurrection, though retired from primary to secondary rank, seems to be waiting rather for clarification by further knowledge. Something of an objective nature certainly lies at its basis; something of an external sort, not the product of mere imagination, took place. To the fact thus indefinitely stated, that hallowing of Sunday as a day of sacred and joyful observance which is coeval with the earliest traditions, and antedates all records, is an attestation as significant as any monumental marble. No hallucination theory, no gradual rise and growth of hope in the minds of a reflective few, can account for that solid primeval monument. But what occurred, the reality in distinctness from any legendary accretions, we shall be better able to conclude, when the truth shall have been threshed out concerning the reality, at present strongly attested, and as strongly controverted, of certain extraordinary but occult psychical powers. (Could it have been only an apparition? The "census of hallucinations" conducted some ten years since by the Society for Psychical Research evinced the reality of veridical apparitions of deceased persons at or near the time of their death, showing the number of verified cases to be so large as to exclude the supposition of chance hallucination (see *Proceedings*, August, 1894). Or could it have been a material body suddenly becoming visible in a closed room, as narrated by Luke and John? First-class evidence, if there can be any such for such occurrences, has been exhibited for such phenomena as the passage of solid substances through intervening doors and walls easy enough, say mathematicians, for a being familiar with the "fourth dimension" and of the levitation of heavy bodies without physical support. (See *Proceedings*, January, 1894, and March,

MIRACLES AND SUPERNATURAL RELIGION

1895.) As to such things skepticism is doubtless in order, but dogmatic contradiction is not. *Sub judice lis est.*)

A point of high significance for those who would cultivate a religious faith not liable to be affected by changes of intellectual outlook or insight is, that this lower valuation of miracle observable among Christian thinkers has not been reached through breaches made by skeptical doubts of the reality of a supernatural Revelation. They have, of course, felt the reasonableness of the difficulties with which traditional opinions have been encumbered by the advance of knowledge. But so far from giving way thereupon to doubts of the reality of divine Revelation, they have sought and found less assailable defenses for their faith in it than those that sufficed their fathers. And their satisfaction therewith stands in no sympathy with those who hold it a mark of enlightenment to assume with Matthew Arnold, that "miracles do not happen." It has resulted rather from reaching the higher grounds of religious thought, on which supernatural Revelation is recognized in its essential character as distinctively moral and spiritual.

The true supernatural is the spiritual, not the miraculous, a higher order of Nature, not a contradiction of Nature. The Revelation of Jesus was altogether spiritual. It consisted in the ideas of God which he communicated by his ministry and teaching, by his character and life. But this, the real supernatural, was not obvious as such to his contemporaries. They looked for it in the lower region of physical effects. And here the Church also in its embryonic spiritual life, in its proneness to externalize religion in forms of rite, and creed, and organization, has thought to find it Jesus' reproof, "Except ye see signs and wonders ye will not believe," is still pertinent to those who will not have it that the supernatural Revelation spiritual though it be can be recognized or believed in apart from an acknowledgment of attendant miracles, wrought in physical nature by an intervention

47

of God. Such a contention, however, is as futile and desperate as was John Wesley's declaration, "The giving up of witchcraft is in effect the giving up of the Bible." Such mischievous fallacies succeed only in blinding many a mind to the real issue which the moral and spiritual Revelation of Jesus makes with men of the twentieth century. It is these fallacies, and not their critics, that create the most of skepticism. (Professor Borden P. Bowne has thus exhibited this great mistake and its grievous consequence: "In popular thought, religious and irreligious alike, the natural is supposed to be something that runs itself without any internal guidance or external interference. The supernatural, on the other hand, if there be any such thing, is not supposed to manifest itself through the natural, but by means of portents, prodigies, interpositions, departures from, or infractions of, natural law in general. The realm of law belongs to the natural, and the natural runs itself. Hence, if we are to find anything supernatural, we must look for it in the abnormal, the chaotic, the lawless, or that which defies all reduction to order that may be depended on. This notion underlies the traditional debate between naturalism and supernaturalism... This unhappy misconception of the relation of the natural to the supernatural has practically led the great body of uncritical thinkers into the grotesque inversion of all reason the more law and order, the less God." *Zions Herald*, August 22, 1900.)

But while the question whether miracles are credible has ceased to be of vital importance, it has by no means lost all importance. On the contrary, so long as the path of progress is guided by the lamp of experience, so long will it be of consequence that the historical record of experience be found trustworthy. It may suit the overweening pride which defies both the past and the present to say with Bonaparte, that history is only a fable that men have agreed to believe. But it is a human interest, and a satisfaction of normal minds to establish, so far as reason permits, the credibility of every record ostensibly historic.

MIRACLES AND SUPERNATURAL RELIGION

To discover that ancient experiences, once supposed to be miraculous raisings from real death, may reasonably be classed with well attested experiences of to-day, better understood as resuscitations from a deathlike trance, should be welcomed by unprejudiced historical critics, as redeeming portions of the ancient record from mistaken disparagement as legendary. That further study may accredit as facts, or at least as founded on facts, some other marvels in that record cannot, except by arrant dogmatism, be pronounced improbable. Nevertheless, it cannot be expected that the legendary element, which both the Old and the New Testament in greater and less degree exhibit, can ever be eliminated.

Such stories as that of the origin of languages at Babel, and that of the resurrection of ancient saints at Jesus' resurrection are indubitable cases of it. But the legendary element, though permanent, is at present undefined. To define it is the problem of the critical student, a problem most difficult to him whose judgment is least subjective ; and he will welcome every contribution that advancing knowledge can supply. Regarding miracle as the natural product of exceptionally endowed life, there is no source from which more light can be shed on its Biblical record than in those studies of the exceptional phenomena and occult powers of life which are prosecuted by the Society for Psychical Research, whose results are recorded in its published Proceedings. For those familiar with this record the legendary element in the Bible tends to shrink into smaller compass than many critics assign it. In the interest both of the Bible and of science it is regrettable that the results of these researches, though conducted by men of high eminence in the scientific world, still encounter the same hostile skepticism even from some Christian believers that Hume directed against the Biblical miracles.

Mr. Gladstone has put himself on record against this

philistinism, saying that "psychical research is by far the most important work that is being done in the world." Were one disposed to prophesy, very reasonable grounds could be produced for the prediction that, great as was the advance of the nineteenth century in physical knowledge, the twentieth century will witness an advance in psychical knowledge equally great. In this advance one may not unreasonably anticipate that some, at least, of the Biblical miracles may be relieved from the skepticism that now widely discredits them.

MIRACLES AND SUPERNATURAL RELIGION

VIII

SYNOPSIS. The cardinal point in the present discussion, the reality not of miracles but of the supernatural. Fallacy of pointing to physical events as essential characteristics of supernatural Revelation. The character of a revelation determined not by its circumstances, but by its contents. Moral nature supernatural to physical. Nature a hierarchy of natures. Supernatural Religion historically attested by the moral development it generates. Transfer of its distinctive note from moral ideals to physical marvels a costly error. Jesus' miracles a revelation, of a type common with others before and since. The unique Revelation of Jesus was in the higher realm of divine ideas and ideals. These, while unrealized in human life, still exhibit the fact of a supernatural Revelation. The distinction of natural and supernatural belongs to the period of moral progress up to the spiritual maturity of man in the image of God. The divine possibilities of humanity, imaged in Jesus, revealed as our inheritance and our prize.

It remains finally to emphasize the point of cardinal importance in the considerations that have been presented. This is not the reality of miracles, but the reality of the supernatural, what it really is, as distinct from what it has been thought to be. The advance of science and philosophy has brought to the front this question; "Have those who reject the claims of supernatural Religion been misinformed as to what it is? Is it, as they have been told, dependent for its attestation on signs and wonders occurring in the sphere of the senses? Does it require acceptance of these, as well as of its teachings? Or is its characteristic appeal wholly to the higher nature of man, relying for its attestation on the witness borne to it by this, rather than by extraordinary phenomena presented to the senses? There is at present no intellectual interest of Christianity more urgent than this; to

51

present to minds imbued with modern learning the true conception of the supernatural and of supernatural Religion.

Miracles, legitimately viewed as the natural product of extraordinary psychical power, or, to phrase it otherwise, of an exceptional vital endowment, belong not to the Hebrew race alone, nor did they cease when the last survivor of the Jewish apostles of Christianity passed away at the end of the first century. This traditional opinion ought by this time to have been entombed together with its long defunct relative, which represented this globe as the fixed center of the revolving heavens. Miracles have the same universality as human life. Nor will their record be closed till the evolution of life is complete. Animal life, advancing through geologic eons to the advent of man, in him reached its climax. Spiritual life, appearing in him as a new bud on an old stock, is evidently far from its climax still. To believe in miracles, as rightly understood, is to believe in spirit and life, and in further unfoldings of their still latent powers.

This, however, is just now of subordinate importance. The present interest of chief moment is a riddance of the hoary fallacy that vitiates the current idea of a supernatural Revelation by looking for its specific characteristics to the physical world. By this deplorable fallacy Christian theology has blinded the minds of many scientific men to the essential claims of Christianity, with immense damage in the arrested development of their religious nature through the skepticism inevitably but needlessly provoked by this great mistake. When Elijah proclaims to idolaters that their deity is no God, and, as we read, corroborates his words by calling down fire from heaven to consume his sacrifice, it is reckoned as supernatural Revelation. But it is not so reckoned when the sage in the book of Proverbs proclaims to a nation of religious formalists the moral character of God: "To do righteousness and justice is more acceptable to the LORD than sacrifice."

This is accounted as ethical teaching, somewhat in advance of the times. A pagan rather than a Christian way of thinking is discoverable here. In each of the cases cited the specific character of supernatural Revelation is equally evident, the disclosure of spiritual truth above the natural thought of the natural men to whom it came. The character of any revelation is determined by the character of the truth made known, not by the drapery of circumstances connected with the making known. Clothes do not make the man, though coarse or careless people may think so. What belongs to the moral and spiritual order is supernatural to what belongs to the material and physical order. This way of thinking will be forced on common minds by thoughtful observation of common things. Animate nature of the lowest rank, as in the grass, is of a higher natural order than inanimate nature in the soil the grass springs from. Sentient nature, as in the ox, is of a higher order than the non-sentient in the grass.

Self-conscious and reflective nature in the man is of a higher order than the selfless and non-reflective nature in his beast of burden. In the composite being of man all these orders of nature coexist, and each higher is supernatural to the nature below it. Nature, the comprehensive term for all that comes into being, is a hierarchy of natures, rising rank above rank from the lowest to the highest. The highest nature known to us, supernatural to all below it, can only be the moral nature, whose full satisfaction is necessary to the highest satisfaction of a man, and in whose complete development only can be realized in permanency his perfected welfare as a social being.

Now it is precisely in the progress of moral development that supernatural Religion manifests itself as a reality. Religion, indeed, is as natural to man as Art. But there is religion and

MIRACLES AND SUPERNATURAL RELIGION

Religion, as there is art and Art the sexual religion of the
primitive Semites, the animistic religion of China, the spiritual
Religion that flowered on the Mount of the Beatitudes,
embryonic religion and Religion adult; all, indeed, natural, yet of
lower and of higher grade. Doubtless, Religion of whatever
grade outranks all other human activities by its distinctive
aspiration to transcend the bounds of space and time and sense,
and to link the individual to the universal; and so all Religion
sounds, feebly or distinctly, the note of the supernatural. But
this is the resonant note of the spiritual Religion which unfolds
in the moral progress of the world. As moral nature is
supernatural to the psychical and the physical, so is its
consummate bloom of spiritual Religion to be ranked as such,
relatively to the religions which more or less dimly and blindly
are yearning and groping toward the light that never was on sea
or land.

Thus defining the word according to the nature of the
thing, supernatural Religion, with its corollary of supernatural
Revelation not as an apparition from without, but as an unfolding
from within, is both a fact and a factor in the development of
spiritual man. The term supernatural Religion has been rightly
applied to that system of religious conceptions, ideals, and
motives, whose effective culture of the moral nature
is attested historically by a moral development superior to the
product of any other known religion. Whether the greatest saints
of Christianity are all of them whiter souls than any that can be
found among the disciples of any other religion, may be matter
for argument. There can be no gainsaying the fact that, of great
and lowly together, no other religion shows so many saints, or
has so advanced the general moral development in lands where
it is widely followed. But its essential character has been
obscured, its appeal to man's highest nature foiled, and its power
lamed by the wretched fallacy that has transferred its distinctive
note of the supernatural from its divine ideals to the physical

marvels embedded in the record of its original promulgation, even conditioning its validity and authority upon their reality.

Such is the false issue which, to the discredit of Christianity, theology has presented to science. Such is the confusion of ideas that in the light of modern knowledge inevitably blocks the way to a reasonable religious faith in multitudes of minds thereby offended. From this costly error Christian theology at length shows signs that it is about to extricate itself. ("Upon the conception of the supernatural as the personal," says Professor Nash, "apologetics must found the claims of Christianity." *Ethics and Revelation*.)

As to the Christian miracles, there can be no reasonable doubt that "mighty works," deemed by many of his contemporaries superhuman, were wrought by Jesus. These, whatever they were, must be regarded as the natural effluence of a transcendentally endowed life. Taking place in the sphere of the senses, they were a revelation of the type seen before and since in the lives of wonder-workers ancient and modern, in whom the power of mind over matter, however astonishing and mysterious, is recognized as belonging to the natural order of things no less than the unexplored Antarctic belongs to the globe. But the Revelation which he gave to human thought as a new thing, a heavenly vision unprecedented, was in the higher realm of the moral and spiritual life. This was the true supernatural, whose reality and power are separable from all its environment of circumstances, and wholly independent thereof. The characteristic ideals of Jesus, his profound consciousness of God, his filial thought of God, his saturation with the conviction of his moral oneness with God. (The words in which Jesus expresses this are much more extraordinary and profoundly significant than any of those mighty works of his the like of which are recorded of the ancient prophets. Jesus was conscious of God as living in him, and of himself as living in God, in the unity of the one eternal life. Not merely as a man of God, but as a man in God, as no other man has consciously been, does Jesus utter such sayings as, "I am the light of the world", "I and my Father are one." (See *Jesus the Ideal Man*, by the present writer. The New World, June, 1897.)) His realization of brotherhood with the meanest human being, still transcend the common level of natural humanity even among his disciples. As thus transcendent they are supernatural still. Till reached and realized, they manifest the fact of a supernatural Revelation in that peerless life as plainly as the sun is manifest in the splendor of a cloudless day. In the coming but distant age, when man's spiritual nature, now so embryonic, shall have become adult, it will doubtless so pervade and rule the physical and psychical natures which it inhabits that the distinction between natural and supernatural, so important in the period of its development, will become foreign alike to thought and speech. But until the making of man in the image of God is complete, when the spiritual element in our composite being, now struggling for development, shall be manifest in its ultimate maturity and ascendancy as the distinctive and proper nature of humanity, it is of supreme importance for the Christian teacher, who would point and urge to the heights of being, to free men's minds of error as to what the real supernatural is. Not the fancied disturber of the world's ordered harmonies, but that highest Nature which is the molder, the glory, and the crown of all the lower. Imaged to us in the human perfectness of Jesus, the ideal Son of man, it is revealed as the distinctive inheritance and prize of the humanity that essays to think the thoughts and walk the ways of God. To each of us is it given in germ by our human birth, to be fostered and nourished in converse with the Infinite Presence that inhabits all things, till its divine possibilities appear in the ultimate "of the sons of God" (Romans viii. 19.) full grown "according to the measure of the stature of the fullness of Christ." (Ephesians iv. 13.)

THE END

CPSIA information can be obtained
at www.ICGtesting.com
Printed in the USA
LVHW081342150319
610795LV00036B/832/P

9 781090 310019